HYMNS OF WORSHIP AND PRAISE

Easy Arrangements for Solo Piano

Arranged by Tim Doran

KANSAS CITY, MO 64141

CONTENTS

Holy, Holy, Holy! Lord God Almighty

JOHN B. DYKES
Arranged by Tim Doran

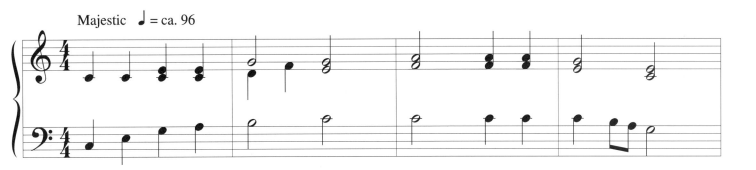

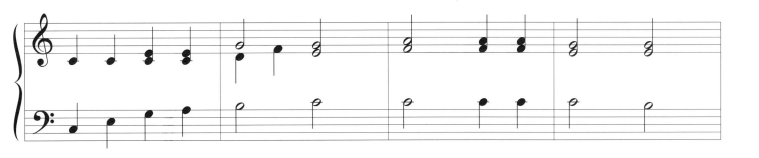

Jesus Loves Me

WILLIAM B. BRADBURY
Arranged by Tim Doran

Gently ♩ = ca. 96

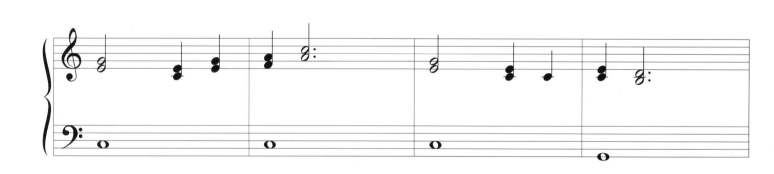

I Sing the Mighty Power of God

Gesangbuch der Herzogl
Arranged by Tim Doran

Majestic ♩ = ca. 112

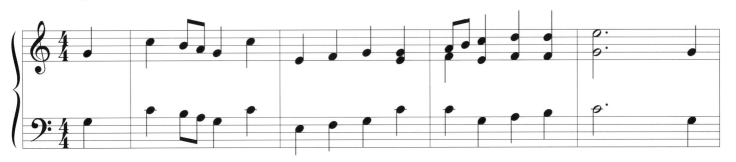

Come, Thou Fount of Every Blessing

Traditional
Arranged by Tim Doran

Flowing ♩ = ca. 96

When Morning Gilds the Skies

JOSEPH BARNBY
Arranged by Tim Doran

Brightly ♩ = ca. 112

Stand Up, Stand Up for Jesus

GEORGE J. WEBB
Arranged by Tim Doran

With conviction ♩ = ca. 112

O Sacred Head, Now Wounded

HANS LEO HASSLER
Arranged by Tim Doran

Moderate ♩ = ca. 96

Rock of Ages

THOMAS HASTINGS
Arranged by Tim Doran

Eternal Father, Strong to Save

JOHN B. DYKES
Arranged by Tim Doran

Majestic ♩ = ca. 96

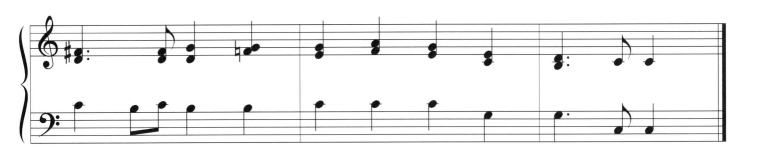

Now Thank We All Our God

JOHANN CRUEGER
Arranged by Tim Doran

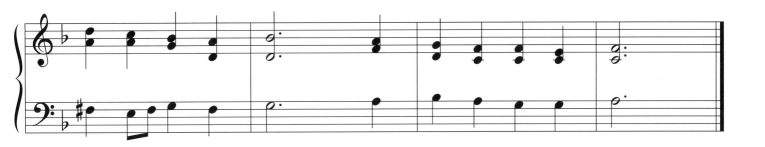

O God, Our Help in Ages Past

WILLIAM CROFT
Arranged by Tim Doran

Moderate ♩ = ca. 96

This Is My Father's World

Traditional
Arranged by Tim Doran

Jesus Shall Reign

JOHN HATTON
Arranged by Tim Doran

Glorious Things of Thee Are Spoken

FRANZ JOSEPH HAYDN
Arranged by Tim Doran

My Jesus, I Love Thee

ADONIRAM J. GORDON
Arranged by Tim Doran

Gently ♩ = ca. 96

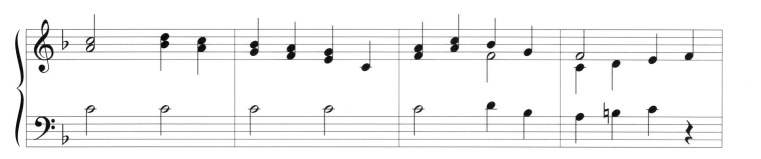

When I Survey the Wondrous Cross

LOWELL MASON
Arranged by Tim Doran

With emotion ♩ = ca. 96

My Faith Has Found a Resting Place

Norwegian Folk Melody
Arranged by Tim Doran

Come, Ye Thankful People, Come

GEORGE J. ELVEY
Arranged by Tim Doran

O for a Thousand Tongues to Sing

CARL G. GLASER
Arranged by Tim Doran

Brightly ♩ = ca. 96

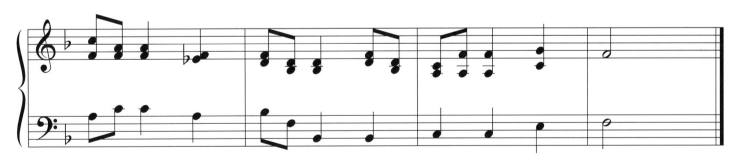

Joyful, Joyful, We Adore Thee

LUDWIG VAN BEETHOVEN
Arranged by Tim Doran

With energy ♩ = ca. 120

Fairest Lord Jesus

Schlesische Volkslieder
Arranged by Tim Doran

Softly ♩ = ca. 88

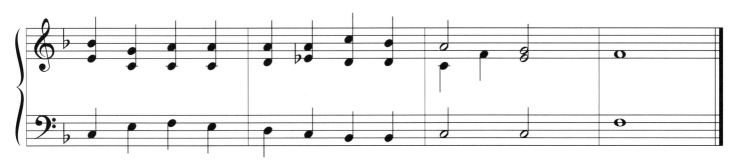

Rejoice, Ye Pure in Heart

ARTHUR H. MESSITER
Arranged by Tim Doran

O Worship the King

JOHANN MICHAEL HAYDN
Arranged by Tim Doran

Majestic ♩ = ca. 112

Praise to the Lord, the Almighty

Stralsund Gesangbuch
Arranged by Tim Doran

Majestic ♩ = ca. 104

Praise God, from Whom All Blessings Flow

LOUIS BOURGEOIS
Arranged by Tim Doran

Moderate ♩ = ca. 96

All Hail the Power of Jesus' Name

OLIVER HOLDEN
Arranged by Tim Doran

Majestic ♩ = ca. 112

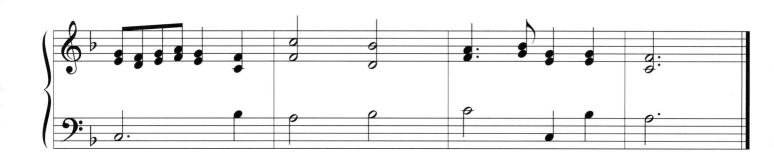

Amazing Grace

Virginia Harmony
Arranged by Tim Doran

Gently ♩ = ca. 96

For the Beauty of the Earth

CONRAD KOCHER
Arranged by Tim Doran

Come, Thou Almighty King

FELICE DE GIARDINI
Arranged by Tim Doran

Majestic ♩ = ca. 120

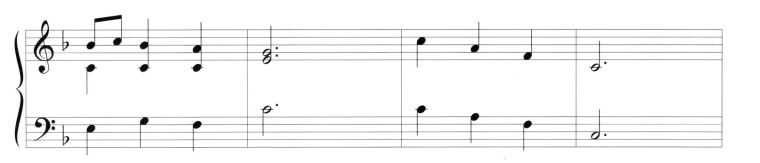

Come, Christians, Join to Sing

Traditional
Arranged by Tim Doran

With conviction ♩ = ca. 120

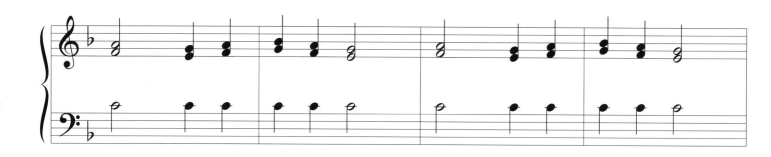

Immortal, Invisible, God Only Wise

Welsh Hymn Tune
Arranged by Tim Doran

Guide Me, O Thou Great Jehovah

JOHN HUGHES
Arranged by Tim Doran

Majestic ♩ = ca. 112

Nearer, My God, to Thee

LOWELL MASON
Arranged by Tim Doran

Softly ♩ = ca. 96

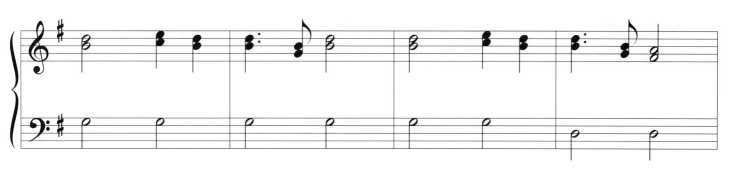

Sun of My Soul

Katholisches Gesangbuch
Arranged by Tim Doran

Moderate   ♩ = ca. 96

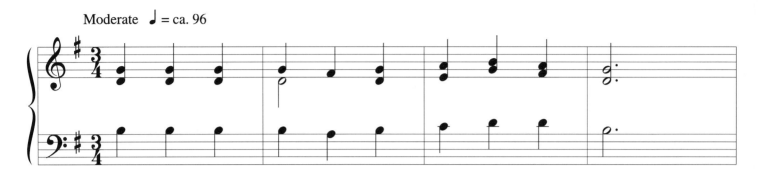

Jesus, Thou Joy of Loving Hearts

HENRY BAKER
Arranged by Tim Doran

Gently ♩ = ca. 96

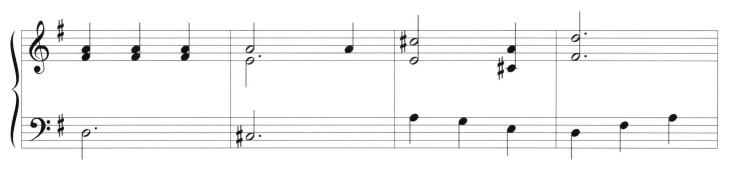